LET'S FIND OUT! *BIOMES*

WHAT ARE TROPICAL RAINFORESTS?

MADDIE GIBBS

Britannica®
Educational Publishing

IN ASSOCIATION WITH

ROSEN
EDUCATIONAL SERVICES

Published in 2019 by Britannica Educational Publishing (a trademark of Encyclopædia Britannica, Inc.) in association with The Rosen Publishing Group, Inc.
29 East 21st Street, New York, NY 10010

Distributed exclusively by Rosen Publishing.
To see additional Britannica Educational Publishing titles, go to rosenpublishing.com.

First Edition

Britannica Educational Publishing
J.E. Luebering: Executive Director, Core Editorial
Mary Rose McCudden: Editor, Britannica Student Encyclopedia

Rosen Publishing
Amelie von Zumbusch: Editor
Matt Cauli: Series Designer
Tahara Anderson: Book Layout
Cindy Reiman: Photography Manager
Sherri Jackson: Photo Researcher

Library of Congress Cataloging-in-Publication Data

Names: Gibbs, Maddie, author.
Title: What are tropical rainforests? / Maddie Gibbs.
Description: First edition. | New York : Britannica Educational Publishing, in Association with Rosen Educational Services, 2019. | Series: Let's find out! Biomes | Includes bibliographical references and index. | Audience: Grades 1–5.
Identifiers: LCCN 2018018984| ISBN 9781508106975 (library bound) | ISBN 9781508107118 (pbk.) | ISBN 9781508107323 (6 pack)
Subjects: LCSH: Rain forests—Juvenile literature. | Rain forest ecology—Juvenile literature.
Classification: LCC QH86 .G53 2019 | DDC 577.34—dc23
LC record available at https://lccn.loc.gov/2018018984

Manufactured in the United States of America

Photo credits: Cover and interior pages background Quick Shot/Shutterstock.com; p. 4 Cyril Ruoso/Minden Pictures/Getty Images; p. 5 Glen Allison/Getty Images; p. 6 Caroline von Tuempling/The Image Bank/Getty Images; p. 7 Claus Meyer/Minden Pictures/Getty Images; pp. 8, 11 © Encyclopædia Britannica, Inc.; p. 9 Alexander Mazurkevich/Shutterstock.com; p. 10 © Dinkum; p. 12 Mike Hill/Stockbyte/Getty Images; p. 13 Robert Lessmann/Shutterstock.com; p. 14 Andrey Nosik/Shutterstock.com; p. 15 © E.R. Degginger; p. 16 Perfect Lazybones/Shutterstock.com; p. 17 © hotshotsworldwide/Fotolia; p. 18 Roy Toft/National Geographic Image Collection/Getty Images; p. 19 © Z. Leszczynski/Animals Animals; p. 20 Education Images/Universal Images Group Editorial/Getty Images; p. 21 Yvan Cohen/LightRocket/Getty Images; p. 22 Pete Oxford/Minden Pictures /Getty Images; p. 23 © Stuart Taylor/Fotolia; p. 24 Urbanhearts/Fotolia; p. 25 © Christopher Meder/Fotolia; p. 26 © Stockbyte/Thinkstock; p. 27 Mark Carwardine/Photolibrary/Getty Images; p. 28 Colin McPherson/Corbis Entertainment/Getty Images; p. 29 Dr. Morley Read/Shutterstock.com.

CONTENTS

THE FOREST BIOMES

Tropical rainforests are one of Earth's biomes. A biome is a large region of Earth that has a certain climate and certain types of living things. Major biomes include tundra, forests, grasslands, and deserts.

There are several forest biomes. The taiga is a conifer forest biome, found in cold northern areas. Deciduous forests are found mainly in the Northern Hemisphere, south of the taiga, but north of tropical forests. Deciduous

◀◀ Gorillas are one of the many kinds of animals that live in tropical rainforests.

COMPARE AND CONTRAST

What do tropical rainforests have in common with other types of forests? In what ways are they different?

forests have four seasons and lose their leaves in the fall.

Thick forests found in wet areas of the world are called rainforests. There are several kinds of rainforests. Temperate rainforests grow in cool parts of the world, such as the northwestern United States and southern Australia. Monsoon rainforests have a dry season and trees that shed their leaves each year. They grow in Southeast Asia. Montane

Washington State has large areas of temperate rainforest.

rainforests, or cloud forests, grow in mountainous regions.

The most familiar rainforests are hot, tropical forests filled with trees that stay green year-round. Tropical rainforests lie near the **equator**. This biome has hot, wet conditions all year

Toucans live in the tropical rainforests of Central and South America.

long. Tall, tropical trees and many other plants grow there. Tropical rainforests are known for the diversity of their plants and animals. Scientists think that more than half of the world's plant and animal species, or types, live in tropical rainforests. There may be many of these species that have not yet been discovered. Monkeys, parrots, jaguars, and anaconda snakes are just a few of the many rainforest animals.

The jaguar is the largest cat in the Americas. It is found mainly in the Amazon Rainforest of South America.

WHERE ARE TROPICAL RAINFORESTS?

Tropical rainforests occur near the equator in the hot, wet region called the tropics. They are found in parts of the tropics that get more than 70 inches (180 centimeters) of rain each year.

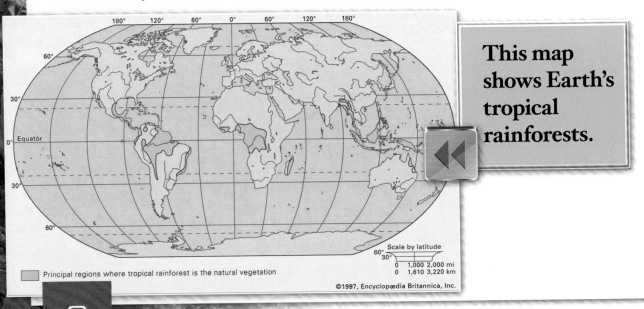

180°   120°   60°   0°   60°   120°   180°

60°

30°

0°   Equator

30°

60°

60°
30°   Scale by latitude

0   1,000   2,000 mi
0   1,610   3,220 km

Principal regions where tropical rainforest is the natural vegetation

©1997, Encyclopædia Britannica, Inc.

This map shows Earth's tropical rainforests.

THINK ABOUT IT
Tropical areas that get less rain are desert and grassland biomes. Why do you think more rain leads to rainforest biomes?

Parts of South America and Central America, western and central Africa, Southeast Asia, and Australia have tropical rainforests. The world's largest rainforest is located in the Amazon River basin of Brazil. It covers about 40 percent of that country. However, tropical rainforests cover less than 5 percent of Earth's total land surface.

The second largest tract of rainforest is in central Africa, in the region around the Congo River. Almost half of the tropical rainforests in this tract are in the Democratic Republic of the Congo. The biggest natural tropical rainforests in Asia are in New Guinea and parts of Borneo.

The world's largest flower can be found in the tropical rainforests of Southeast Asia.

FROM THE CANOPY TO THE GROUND

Tropical rainforests can be divided into several sections. At the top of the forest is a thick layer called the canopy. It is formed by the spreading branches and thick leaves of tall trees. The canopy blocks much of the sunlight from the area below. The canopy can be between 100 and 170 feet (30 and 50 meters) above the ground. A few very tall trees stick up above the rest of the canopy. They are called emergent trees.

Water can be seen in the distance over the canopy of a rainforest in Australia.

THINK ABOUT IT

Why do you think many animals make their homes in the canopy?

Many animals live among the treetops of the canopy. These include insects, birds, and mammals.

The section below the canopy is called the understory. It contains small trees, shrubs, and plants. Many of these are saplings, or young trees. Their stems reach up toward the light. However, these smaller trees generally do not receive enough sunlight to grow into adult trees.

canopy

understory

Different plants grow at different levels in a tropical rainforest.

On the forest floor, it is usually dark because the canopy blocks so much sunlight. Therefore, only plants that can tolerate shade grow there. So little sunlight reaches the ground that the forest floor may be only lightly covered by ground vegetation. There may be open spaces between the tree trunks. If one of the trees that creates the canopy dies or falls, a gap may open in the canopy, allowing sunlight to reach farther down into the forest. In such cases the ground vegetation may become thick and dense.

The constant rain washes away many of

This plant sprouted on the dark floor of a tropical rainforest.

the **nutrients** in the soil. To make up for that loss, bacteria, fungi, and insects on the forest floor help to break down dead plants and animals. This process creates a thin, rich top layer of soil that provides nutrients to the roots of the plants and trees. Because this layer is thin, most of the trees have shallow root systems.

The tall roots growing from the trunk of this Costa Rican rainforest tree are known as buttress roots.

Tropical Rainforest Plants

The trees found in tropical rainforests stay green all year, though they do shed their leaves sometimes. Palms are among the most common trees.

Below the thick canopy, other plants have to compete with each other to get enough light. As a result, many plants use other plants to reach toward the sunlight. For example, woody plants called lianas attach to the stems of other plants and climb from the ground to the canopy. Epiphytes, or air plants, are also

A liana encircles a tree in a rainforest in Australia.

THINK ABOUT IT

Why do you think that epiphytes have been so successful in tropical rainforests? What advantage might there be in not having roots attached to the ground?

abundant in the rainforest. These plants are not attached to the ground. They live on other plants. They get water and minerals from rain and also from debris that collects on the supporting plants. Mosses, ferns, and orchids can often be found attached to larger plants.

These orchids are examples of the type of tropical rainforest plant called an epiphyte.

TROPICAL RAINFOREST ANIMALS

Each area of the rainforest has thousands of species of animals. Many plant-eating animals live in the canopy—for example, monkeys, flying squirrels, and sharp-clawed woodpeckers. At the lower levels of the forest are animals that run, flutter, hop, and climb in the undergrowth.

Orangutans live in tropical rainforests on two islands in Southeast Asia.

On the rainforest floor are such animals as chimpanzees, gorillas, elephants, pigs, deer, and leopards.

COMPARE AND CONTRAST

How is the animal life in tropical rainforests like that in other forests? How is it different?

Many animals in the rainforest have unusual characteristics. For example, sloths hang upside down, resting for hours at a time. The bright colors of the tiny poison dart frog warn other animals that it is poisonous and should not be eaten. Other common animals throughout the forests include ants, beetles, snakes, and bats. There are also many brightly colored birds such as toucans, parrots, and macaws.

Most poison dart frogs are very small.

Spotlight on the Amazon Rainforest

The world's largest rainforest is the Amazon Rainforest. Its plant and animal life is rich. Almost three-fourths of all the plant species in the world grow there.

Mammals include nutria, great anteaters, and many monkey species. The capybara, a rodent that can weigh more than 110 pounds (50 kilograms), lives there. So does the tapir, a hoofed mammal that looks somewhat like a pig. A variety of fish, including the pirarucu—which

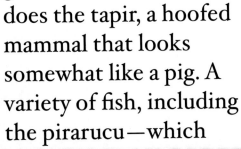

Tapirs are shy animals that like the deep forest. They are most active at night.

THINK ABOUT IT

Why do you think the Amazon Rainforest has so much diversity?

weighs up to 325 pounds (150 kg)—and the giant catfish, swim in the river. Silver carp, neon tetras, and flesh-eating piranhas are shipped to tropical fish stores throughout the world. The electric eel is a dangerous fish capable of discharging up to 500 volts.

Hummingbirds, toucans, and parrots are among the many colorful Amazonian birds. Reptiles include the anaconda (a huge snake that crushes its victims), the poisonous coral snake, and alligators. Giant butterflies are among the most spectacular of the insects.

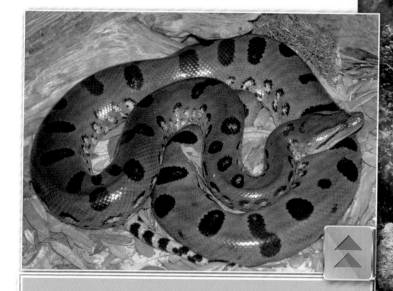

The giant, or green, anaconda is the largest snake in the world.

Rainforest Peoples

Rainforests have been home to tribal peoples for thousands of years. These include the Yanomami and the Kayapó of the Amazon Rainforest, the Bambuti of the Ituri Forest of central Africa, the Kombai in Indonesia, and the Penan in Malaysia.

Many rainforest peoples were forced to move or to change their way of life as they came into contact with people from the outside world. However, there are still some groups that have maintained their

This Yanomami hunter is using a traditional bow to hunt in the canopy.

traditional culture. There are still others that are considered "uncontacted," or undiscovered. These are people who are located so remotely that they have yet to be encountered or who have intentionally been left alone by outsiders.

Human rights organizations have called on governments and the companies that operate in the rainforests to protect the rights of the native peoples in these areas. Some countries have set aside protected areas for the tribes to live in, but conflicts continue.

A Kelabit activist (*right*) speaks with a Penan couple. The Penan and Kelabit are both rainforest peoples.

An Important Biome

A tropical rainforest is a delicate network of relationships between plants and animals. Many plants, for instance, rely on animals to spread their **pollen** from flower to flower. At the same time, animals may depend on plants for their food and shelter. In addition, millions of people live in the forests. For them the forests are sources of food, shelter, and other materials.

Even people who live far away from tropical rainforests are affected by the forests. Many

Macaws depend on their tropical rainforest home for food.

rainforest plants are used as medicines to help treat diseases. Quinine, which is used to fight malaria, comes from rainforest plants. So does paclitaxel, which is used to fight some cancers. Scientists believe there are many more plants there that will help treat or even cure serious diseases. In addition, products such as fruits, nuts, rubber, rattan, and wood come from rainforests.

People collect the milky sap from rubber trees. It is called latex and is used to make rubber. ▶▶

Tropical rainforests also help to control the water supply of the areas where they grow. They do this by absorbing the constant rain and then releasing it slowly back into the atmosphere. Some of the water is released steadily into rivers. Many people rely on the rivers for their water supply and to irrigate their crops. Some of the water is released back into the air through evaporation. This keeps the air moist and leads to more rain. This important process is called the **water cycle**.

Finally, like all green plants, rainforest plants absorb carbon dioxide gas from the atmosphere and produce oxygen. They do this

The Amazon River is one of several major rivers that wind through rainforests.

through the process of photosynthesis. Because the number of plants in the rainforests is so huge, the forests produce much of the world's oxygen, which all animals need to live. For this reason, tropical rainforests have been called the "lungs of the planet."

VOCABULARY

The **water cycle** is the continuous movement of Earth's water through the air, on land, and in the ground.

Rainforests, such as this one in Malaysia, are among Earth's major sources of oxygen.

THE DESTRUCTION OF TROPICAL RAINFORESTS

Tropical rainforests grow in many poor countries. Some poor countries sell the wood and other resources of rainforests to make much-needed money. This often means that entire sections of the forest are destroyed. Rainforests are also cut down so that the land can be used for other purposes, such as cattle grazing and farming. The rainforests that are destroyed for these

The Amazon Rainforest has greatly declined because of slash-and-burn farming.

reasons are rarely replaced.

Slash-and-burn agriculture is common in rainforest areas. It consists of cutting trees and other vegetation, burning what is left, and then planting crops. Because of poor soil, many such areas can support only two or three agricultural plantings. After that the soil's nutrients are exhausted and the land is abandoned.

The loss of rainforests endangers many plants and animals that live nowhere else in the world. Over time,

COMPARE AND CONTRAST

What does slash-and-burn agriculture have in common with the cutting down of rainforests? How might its effects be different?

The Sumatran rhinoceros is an endangered rainforest animal.

27

some of these plants and animals may become extinct if their rainforest habitat is destroyed.

When rainforests are cleared, the water cycle is disrupted as well. Rainwater washes away quickly instead of being stored in the plants and returned slowly to the atmosphere. Eventually, rain falls less often, and the region may experience drought.

The destruction of rainforests also affects the environment of the rest of the world. When forests are burned, massive amounts of carbon dioxide escape into the atmosphere. This carbon dioxide contributes to a problem known as global warming. Global warming is

This stretch of the Amazon Rainforest has been cleared. Rainforest destruction has both local and global effects.

the gradual rise in Earth's average surface temperature. It happens because the extra greenhouse gases—such as carbon dioxide—that people have added to Earth's atmosphere trap in extra heat.

Cutting down rainforests also contributes to global warming in another way. Trees use carbon dioxide when they make their own food. Fewer trees mean that less carbon dioxide is being taken out of the atmosphere.

Conserving tropical rainforests is one of several steps people can take to fight global warming.

GLOSSARY

absorb To take in or suck or swallow up.

atmosphere The layer of gas that surrounds Earth.

bacteria Tiny living things that can be found in all natural environments and consist of a single cell.

cancer A disease that causes certain cells in the body to grow out of control.

carbon dioxide A gas that animals breathe out and plants use in photosynthesis.

climate The weather found in a certain place over a long period of time.

debris The remains of something broken down or destroyed.

diversity A mix or range of different things; variety.

drought A shortage of rain over a long period of time.

extinct No longer existing.

fern A flowerless green plant with leaves that look like feathers.

fungi A group of simple living things that are neither plants nor animals. Mushrooms, molds, and yeasts are fungi.

irrigate To supply with water by artificial means.

malaria A serious disease spread by mosquitoes.

mammal A type of living thing with a backbone and fur or hair. Female mammals produce milk to feed their babies.

moss A small, seedless plant that often grows in moist, shady places.

oxygen A gas that animals need to breathe and plants produce during photosynthesis.

photosynthesis The process in which green plants use sunlight to make their own food.

rattan Stems from a climbing palm that are used to make furniture and baskets.

temperate Having a climate that is usually mild without extremely cold or extremely hot temperatures.

tract A large stretch of land.

vegetation Plant life or cover.

FOR MORE INFORMATION

Books

Clarke, Ginjer L. *Life in the Amazon Rainforest.* New York, NY: Penguin Young Readers, 2018.

Hyde, Natalie. *Amazon Rainforest Research Journal* (Ecosystems Research Journal). New York, NY: Crabtree Publishing Company, 2018.

Llewellyn, Claire. *Mysterious Rain Forests: Come Face to Face with Life in the Rain Forest* (Fast Facts). New York, NY: Kingfisher, 2016.

Spilsbury, Louise, and Richard Spilsbury. *Forest Biomes.* New York, NY: Crabtree Publishing, 2018.

Wood, John. *Animals in the Rain Forest.* New York, NY: KidHaven Publishing, 2018.

Websites

Arizona State University: Ask a Scientist
https://askabiologist.asu.edu/explore/rainforest
Facebook: @Dr.Biology, Twitter: @Drbiology

Kids Do Ecology
http://kids.nceas.ucsb.edu/biomes/rainforest.html

Rainforest Alliance
https://www.rainforest-alliance.org/faqs/what-is-a-rainforest
Facebook: @RainforestAlliance; Twitter: @RnfrstAlliance

World Wildlife Federation
http://wwf.panda.org/about_our_earth/deforestation/importance_forests/tropical_rainforest/
Facebook and Twitter: @WWF

INDEX